NATIONAL GEOGRAPHIC
School Publishing

Shapes

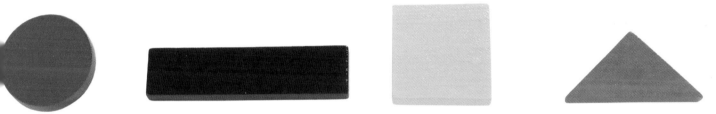

Edward Lincoln

PICTURE CREDITS

Illustration by Marjory Gardner (14–15).
Cover, 2, 4 (above), 5 (center & right), 6 (all), 7 (all), 8 (below right), 9 (all), 10 (left), 11 (below left & above right), 12 (left), Photolibrary.com; 1, 4 (below), 5 (below), Lindsay Edwards Photography; 4 (center), Swerve/Alamy; 5 (above left), Zefa Images; 8 (left), 11 (above left), 12 (below right), 13 (above left, above right & below), Getty Images; 8 (above right), Photodisc.

Produced through the worldwide resources of the National Geographic Society, John M. Fahey, Jr., President and Chief Executive Officer; Gilbert M. Grosvenor, Chairman of the Board; Nina D. Hoffman, Executive Vice President and President, Books and Education Publishing Group.

PREPARED BY NATIONAL GEOGRAPHIC SCHOOL PUBLISHING

Ericka Markman, Senior Vice President and President Children's Books and Education Publishing Group; Steve Mico, Senior Vice President and Publisher; Marianne Hiland, Editorial Director; Lynnette Brent, Executive Editor; Michael Murphy and Barbara Wood, Senior Editors; Bea Jackson, Design Director; David Dumo, Art Director; Margaret Sidlowsky, Illustrations Director; Matt Wascavage, Manager of Publishing Services; Sean Philpotts, Production Manager.

MANUFACTURING AND QUALITY MANAGEMENT

Christopher A. Liedel, Chief Financial Officer; Phillip L. Schlosser, Director; Clifton M. Brown III, Manager.

BOOK DEVELOPMENT

Ibis for Kids Australia Pty Limited.

Published by the National Geographic Society
1145 17th Street, N.W.
Washington, D.C. 20036-4688

ISBN: 0-7922-6058-9

Fifth Printing June 2018
Printed in the USA

Contents

targets

ticket

circle

rectangle

square

4

What shapes do you see in these photos?

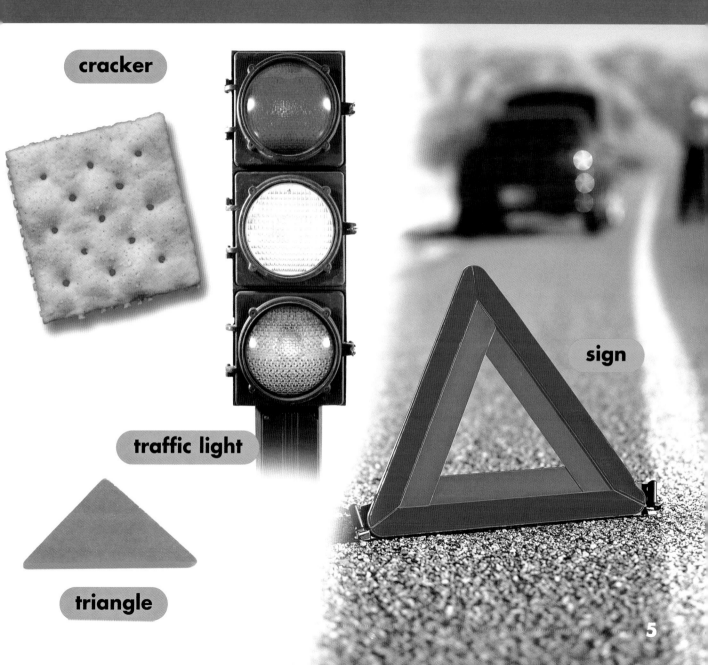

cracker

traffic light

triangle

sign

5

Circles

A circle is a round shape.

Triangles

A triangle has 3 straight sides and 3 corners.

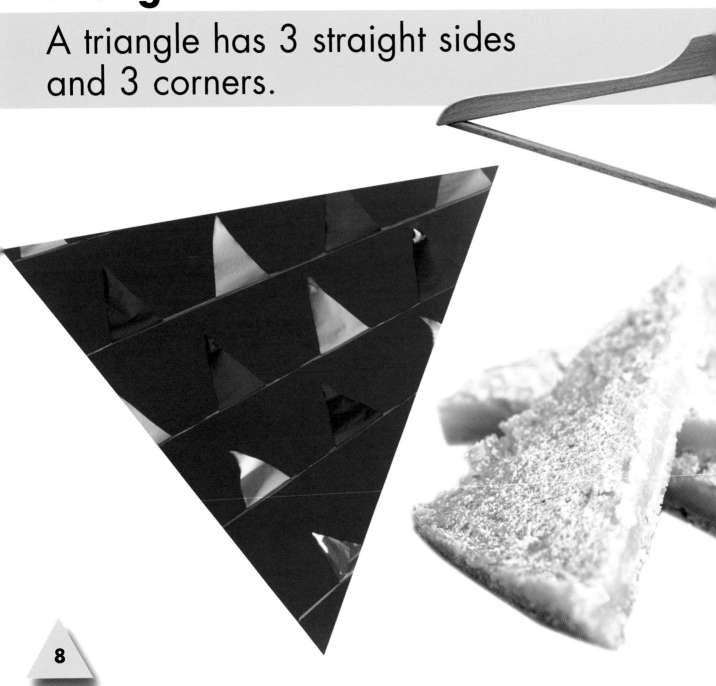

Rectangles

A rectangle has 4 straight sides and 4 corners.

NATIONAL GEOGRAPHIC
Windows on Literacy®

Math in
Social Studies

Flags

Jan Pritchett

Squares

A square is a special rectangle.
Its 4 sides are all the same length.

14

There are many shapes in this picture. Can you find them?

circle

corner

rectangle

round

shape

side

square

triangle

Picture Glossary

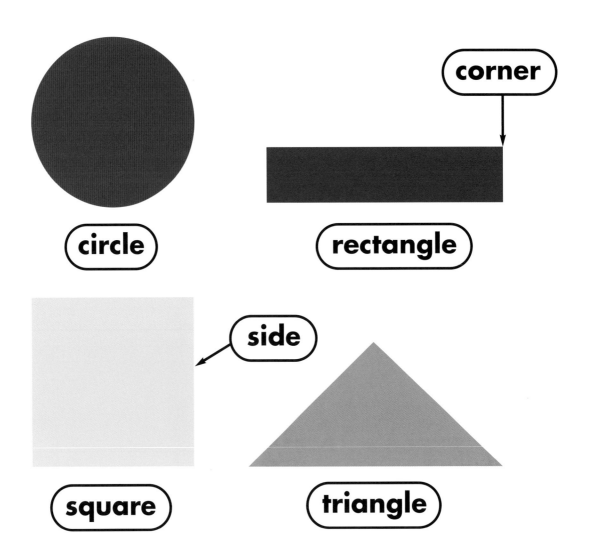

circle

corner

rectangle

side

square

triangle